RORY MCILROY

A Golfing Legend's Remarkable Rise

Melinda C. Bills

Table of Content

Introduction

Chapter 1: The Early Years
Rory's humble beginnings and introduction to golf
His family's influence on his passion for the sport
Early achievements and prodigious talent

Chapter 2: Rising through the Ranks
Junior and amateur career highlights
Transitioning to professional golf
Winning his first major tournament

Chapter 3: The Quest for Major Titles
Rory's pursuit of Grand Slam glory
Iconic victories at the U.S. Open, The Open Championship, etc.
Challenges and setbacks on the path to major success

Chapter 4: The Making of a Golfing Legend
Insights into Rory's training and practice routines

Introduction

In the realm of expert golf, there are not many names as inseparable from ability, assurance, and sheer brightness as Rory McIlroy. A wonder who overwhelmed the hitting the fairway world very early on, McIlroy's journey from a maturing fan on the rich greens of Northern Ireland to a worldwide symbol ruling lofty competitions is downright exceptional.

Destined to swing a club and bound to succeed someday, McIlroy's story isn't only one of donning accomplishments; it's a demonstration of the unflinching soul of a boss. His transient ascent through the positions of novice golf was a simple introduction to the remarkable accomplishments he would achieve on the expert circuit. With a swing as smooth as silk and a psychological courage that matches the legends of the game, McIlroy cut his name into the records of playing golf history, rethinking the game's norms and enrapturing crowds around the world.

In any case, past the impeccably executed shots and the prizes covering his racks, there lies a story of versatility, difficult work, and unshakeable self-conviction. McIlroy's process typifies the substance of persevering pursuit, moving ages of hopeful golf players to think beyond practical boundaries, work harder, and try the impossible.

In this exploration of Rory McIlroy's life, we dive into the core of a golf player who didn't simply play the game; he turned into the game. Go along with us as we unravel the layers of this wonderful competitor, from his unassuming starting points to his victorious minutes on the world stage. This isn't simply a tale about a golf player; it's a story of enthusiasm, devotion, and the relentless quest for greatness. Welcome to the remarkable universe of Rory McIlroy.

Chapter 1: The Early Years

In the picturesque town of Holywood, Northern Ireland, a young boy named Rory McIlroy was introduced to a sport that would become his lifelong passion: golf. This chapter delves into the formative years of one of the most celebrated golfers of his generation, shedding light on the early influences and moments that ignited his love for the game.

Rory's humble beginnings and introduction to golf

Rory McIlroy's journey in golf had its foundations in his modest starting points. Brought into the world on May 4, 1989, in Holywood, Northern Ireland, Rory's initial openness to the game was impacted by his golf-adoring family. His dad, Gerry McIlroy, maintained numerous sources of income to help Rory's maturing ability and desire to play golf.

Rory's most memorable journey to golf came very early in life, around the age of two when he accepted his most memorable golf club. His dad would take him to the close by Holywood Golf Club, where Rory started rehearsing his swing. It immediately became obvious that the little fellow had a characteristic fitness for the game, and he fostered an energy for golf that would characterize his life.

As Rory's advantage and abilities developed, his folks assumed a critical part in sustaining his ability. His mom, Rosie McIlroy, frequently moved him to the fairway and competitions. Rory's devotion was clear from his initial years, and his family's immovable help gave the establishment to his excursion into the universe of expert golf.

In those early stages, Rory's first experience with golf was not just about learning the specialized parts of the game but also about imparting in him a solid hard-working attitude and love for the game. His family's penances and obligation to his fantasy would ultimately prompt Rory to become quite possibly one of the most noticeable figures in the realm of golf.

Rory's modest starting points and first experience with golf act as a demonstration of the force of enthusiasm, family backing, and commitment in shaping the existence of a playing golf legend. This early part in his life laid the foundation for a wonderful profession that would see him make extraordinary progress on the world's golf stage.

His family's influence on his passion for the sport

Rory McIlroy's firmly established enthusiasm for golf can be followed back to the steady help and impact of his loved ones. Experiencing childhood in Holywood, Northern Ireland, Rory was encircled by a family that shared his energy for the game. His dad, Gerry McIlroy, maintained various sources of income to help his child's growing golf profession, frequently forfeiting his own time and assets to guarantee Rory had the best chance to succeed.

Rory's folks perceived his ability and commitment from the beginning. It was his dad, Gerry, who acquainted him with golf, perceiving the little fellow's regular fondness for the game. Gerry turned into Rory's most memorable mentor and tutor, imparting in him the specialized parts of golf as well as the upsides of discipline, constancy, and sportsmanship.

Rory's mom, Rosie, likewise assumed an essential part in sustaining his energy for golf. She offered in-depth help and relief that each hopeful competitor needed. Her attendance at his competitions, whether near junior occasions or worldwide titles, was a wellspring of inspiration for Rory. Her unflinching faith in his capacities supported his certainty and assurance to succeed in the game.

Moreover, Rory's folks established a strong and supporting climate at home. They cultivated his affection for golf by permitting him to rehearse at the nearby Holywood Golf Club and by orchestrating valuable open doors for him to play with experienced golf players, leveling up his abilities and moving him along.

Past close family, Rory's more distant family, and direct relations likewise assumed a part in filling his enthusiasm for golf. Their aggregate confidence in his ability gave him a solid groundwork, empowering him to seek after his fantasies with unflinching assurance.

Rory McIlroy's family perceived his true capacity as well as effectively sustaining his enthusiasm for golf. Their impact formed his abilities as a golf player as well as contributed essentially to the improvement of his personality, making him not entirely set in stone, centered, and humble competitor the world respects today. Their perseverance through help fills in as a demonstration of the force of family in molding the fates of remarkable people.

Early achievements and prodigious talent

From early on, it was obvious that he had an interesting blend of expertise, concentration, and assurance that would move him to fame. The first experience with golf was fortunate, as his dad, Gerry, had taken up the game as a method for holding with his young child. Much to their surprise this presentation would stamp the start of a surprising journey.

When Rory was only 9 years of age, his ability was unquestionable. He brought home the Big showdown for his age bunch and before long turned into the most youthful individual from Hollywood Golf Club. His capacity to drive the ball unimaginable distances and his normal feel for the game were qualities that would turn into his brand name.

As a youngster, McIlroy's standing as a hitting-the-fairway wonder kept on developing. He brought home various beginner championships, remembering the Irish Amateur Close Championship in 2005 and the West Ireland Championship in 2006. His strength in amateur golf finished in his triumph at the 2006 European Beginner Title, an accomplishment that further hardened his huge ability.

In 2007, Rory McIlroy pursued a critical choice to turn proficient at 18 years old. His fast climb in the expert positions was out and out uncommon. In his third expert beginning, he got his most memorable triumph at the 2009 Dubai Desert Classic, reporting his appearance on the global playing golf stage. His childhood, mystique, and the easy way wherein he played the game charmed him to fans all over the planet.

What put McIlroy aside was his actual ability as well as his psychological mettle. He showed a degree of development and self-restraint in past years, permitting him to deal with the tensions of expert golf with momentous beauty.

These early accomplishments in his vocation, set apart by his successes as a youthful novice and his consistent progress into the expert world, foreshadowed the striking achievement that Rory McIlroy would accomplish in the years to come. His monstrous ability was apparent to all who watched him, and he was bound to play golf significance.

Chapter 2: Rising through the Ranks

From his promising junior and amateur career to the cutting-edge minutes in the realm of expert golf, this part reveals the fundamental stages that molded McIlroy into hitting the fairway sensation he is today.

Junior and amateur career highlights

These features are significant sections in the narrative of Rory McIlroy, as they establish the groundwork for his exceptional expert achievement.

In his initial years, Rory McIlroy showed an unprecedented fitness for golf.

Hailing from Holywood, Northern Ireland, youthful Rory started swinging a club before he might walk, and by the age of two, he was at that point showing a tremendous ability for the game. Under the direction of his dad, Gerry McIlroy, who maintained various sources of income to help his child's aspirations, Rory's abilities prospered.

Quite possibly the main early achievement in Rory's lesser career was bringing home the World Golf Title for his age bunch at nine years old. This triumph denoted the start of a series of achievements in junior golf that set up his future as an expert golf player. His commitment to the game was apparent and still, after all that, as he rehearsed enthusiastically, leveling up his abilities on the greens and fairways of neighborhood courses.

As Rory progressed into the beginner positions, he kept on separating himself. He turned into the most youthful victor of the

West Ireland Championship in 2005, and in 2006, he won the esteemed European Beginner Championship. These triumphs showed his capacity to contend at a significant level and were early marks of his true capacity as a future-hitting fairway star.

Notwithstanding, it was Rory's presentation in the 2007 Walker Cup, addressing Extraordinary England and Ireland, that genuinely slung him into the worldwide spotlight. He assumed a vital part in his group's triumph, displaying his exceptional expertise, balance, and seriousness. It was during this time that many started to consider the youthful Irishman with a splendid future in the realm of golf.

Rory McIlroy's lesser and novice profession features were critical in molding the golf player he would turn into. These early triumphs imparted in him a healthy identity conviction and assurance, giving a strong groundwork for his future outcome in proficient golf. His journey from a little fellow swinging a club in Holywood to a beginner champion was only the start of a phenomenal hitting-the-fairway story.

Transitioning to professional golf

The progress from the beginner position to proficient golf is a basic point in the career of any yearning golf player, and Rory McIlroy's process was no special case.

The Choice to Turn Pro

Rory McIlroy's choice to turn expert was impacted by his unquestionable ability and a progression of great accomplishments in the novice circuit. His triumph in the 2005 Irish Novice Close Championship, combined with his appearance in the 2007 Walker Cup, displayed his capability to the golf world. With the backing of his family and tutors, Rory pursued the strong choice to turn proficient in 2007, only days after his eighteenth birthday celebration.

The Early Difficulties

Life as an expert golf player accompanied its arrangement of difficulties. Rory needed to adjust to a seriously requesting plan, stiffer contest, and the tensions of earning enough to pay the bills through golf. The section explores his underlying battles and how he figured out how to drive forward through these early troubles, showing the psychological backbone that would become one of his brand names.

Early Expert Triumphs

Notwithstanding the underlying obstacles, Rory immediately laid down a good foundation for himself as a rising star in proficient golf. He asserted his most memorable triumph on the European Tour in 2009, turning into the most youthful player to win on the tour starting around 1930. The account unfurls as Rory's initial triumphs allude to the significance that lies ahead.

Exploring the Worldwide Stage

One of the one-of-a-kind difficulties Rory faced as an expert was the progress to contending on a worldwide stage. It talks about his encounters on both the European Visit and the PGA Visit, the subtleties of various configurations, and his effective route in these assorted scenes.

Guides and Impacts

All through his progress to proficient golf, Rory was lucky to have the direction and backing of guides and individual experts who gave him important experiences and counsel.

Winning his first major tournament

The occasion that carved his name into the chronicles of golf history was the 2011 U.S. Open, held at Legislative Nation Club in Bethesda, Maryland.

At only 22 years of age, McIlroy showed an uncommon degree of self-restraint and ability all through the competition. He opened with a dazzling round of 65, quickly getting the notice of the playing golf world. As the competition advanced, he kept on ruling the field, expanding his lead with each round.

His stunning presentation finished in an unrivaled triumph. McIlroy wrapped up with an all-out score of 16-under-standard, an eight-stroke edge of triumph, and another U.S. Open scoring record. His accomplishment was a demonstration of his momentous ability as well as his psychological grit and capacity to endure tension on one of the game's most fabulous stages.

The triumph was met with a melody of praise from individual golf players, fans, and savants, who saw in McIlroy the commitment of another period in the game. With his U.S. Open victory, he became perhaps one of the most youthful and significant bosses in golf history, joining the positions of amazing figures like Jack Nicklaus and Tiger Woods.

The success at the 2011 U.S. Open set up Rory McIlroy's transient ascent to the highest point of the golf world. It was a brief look at the significance that was to come in his career, as he proceeded to bring home more significant titles and secure himself as one of the game's most unique and dearest figures. The triumph characterized McIlroy as a notable boss as well as an image of the game's future.

Chapter 3: The Quest for Major Titles

In expert golf, there are not many achievements as desired and respected as significant title titles. For Rory McIlroy, the quest for these lofty triumphs has been a characterizing subject throughout his career.

Rory's pursuit of Grand Slam glory

One of the characterizing sections in Rory McIlroy's famous golf career has been his determined quest for the Grand Slam in professional golf. The Grand Slam alludes to coming out on top for every one of the four significant titles in a golf player's career: The Bosses, the U.S. Open, The Open Championship (frequently alluded to as the British Open), and the PGA Championship.

Rory's journey to join the select club of Grand Slam champions started with his most memorable significant triumph at the U.S. Open in 2011. This success, by a shocking eight-shot edge, was a disclosure of his enormous ability and potential. It set up for what many trusted would be a notable career.

His subsequent significant Championship came at the PGA Championship in 2012, and he followed it up with a bring-home at The Open Championship in 2014. Right now, the hitting the fairway world was dazzled by the possibility of McIlroy finishing the Grand Slam, an accomplishment accomplished by just five different golf players ever.

Be that as it may, the quest for Grand Slam magnificence likewise accompanied its portion of difficulties and heartbreaks. McIlroy got through a baffling period where significant triumphs evaded him. Wounds and variances in structure presented obstacles en route. Golf, as any devotee knows, is a game where even the smallest of changes can have a significant effect.

Rory's momentous versatility and assurance radiated through as he returned from difficulty. He got his second PGA title in 2014, building up his status as one of the game's greats.

Then, in 2019, McIlroy accomplished a critical achievement by coming out on top for The Players Championship, frequently hinted to as golf's informal fifth major. This triumph was viewed as a venturing stone toward finishing the huge home run.

As Rory McIlroy keeps on pursuing his fantasy about joining the tip-top gathering of Grand Slam champions, golf devotees all over the planet anxiously observe each significant title, expecting to observe history taking shape. The quest for Grand Slam brilliance typifies the commitment, energy, and soul of a golf player who has made a permanent imprint on the game and one who remains near the very edge of leaving a mark on the world.

Iconic victories at the U.S. Open, and The Open Championship

Rory McIlroy's career has been accentuated by a few notable triumphs, with his victories at the U.S. Open and The Open Championship standing apart as vital turning points in the realm of golf.

1. U.S. Open (2011): A Cutting edge Execution

Rory McIlroy's victory at the 2011 U.S. Open denoted a defining moment in his career. At only 22 years of age, he exhibited astounding self-control and expertise, overwhelming the field at the Legislative Nation Club in Bethesda, Maryland. His competition execution was out and out awesome, establishing different standards en route. McIlroy's last score of 16-under-standard broke the past U.S. Open record and set another norm for greatness. This made him get his most memorable and significant title and reported his appearance as a potential playing perfectly.

2. The Open Title (2014): The Regal Liverpool Thunder

In 2014, Rory McIlroy added one more significant title to his assortment by coming out on top for The Open Championship at Illustrious Liverpool Golf Club. The triumph was a presentation of his flexibility in various kinds of courses. McIlroy's rounds of 66-66-68-71 were noteworthy as well as steady, featuring his capacity to explore the difficult connections style design. This success at Hoylake denoted his third significant title and set his status as one of the most skilled players of his age.

3. The Open Title (2019): A Sweet Re-visitation of Imperial Portrush

In 2019, Rory McIlroy got back to Imperial Portrush Golf Club in Northern Ireland, where he had established the course standard as a 16-year-old. The homecoming was loaded up with massive tension and assumptions, yet McIlroy embraced the test. He conveyed a charging opening round and, notwithstanding an early difficulty, battled courageously to take care of business and stayed in conflict. While he didn't decisively win the competition, his exhibition and close-to-home home association with the fans made it a remarkable offer in his vocation.

These notorious triumphs at the U.S. Open and The Open Championship grandstand Rory McIlroy's capacity to perform under tension, adjust to various course conditions and concrete his place in hitting the fairway. He comes out on top for adding significant championships to his name as well as having enduring effects on golf aficionados around the world.

Challenges and setbacks on the path to major success

He experienced various difficulties and misfortunes that tested his flexibility, assurance, and mental strength. These obstacles became vital turning points, molding his personality and improving his abilities as a golf player.

One of the critical difficulties McIlroy confronted was taking care of the monstrous strain that accompanies being a wonder. As a youthful golf player, he showed extraordinary ability, and assumptions were high. Adapting to the heaviness of these assumptions and figuring out how to deal with his nerves on the large stage was an extensive test.

Besides, wounds represented a critical difficulty in McIlroy's profession. In the same way as other competitors, he needed to defeat actual sicknesses, for example, back and rib wounds, which sidelined him during critical competitions. Engaging through these wounds required actual restoration as well as mental determination to return more grounded not entirely set in stone.

Another test was adjusting to changes in his game and strategy. Golf is a game that requests persistent improvement, and McIlroy needed to refine his abilities and adjust his playing style to remain cutthroat. This interaction frequently elaborates on working with mentors, changing his swing, and adjusting different parts of his game, which required tolerance and persistence.

Also, McIlroy confronted wild rivalry from other gifted golf players. The hitting the fairway scene is dabbed with uncommon players, each competing for the sought-after significant titles. Conquering rivals and reliably beating them in high-stakes competitions required extraordinary ability as well as mental strength and vital play.

Eventually, the mental test of quickly returning from appalling misfortunes tried McIlroy's psychological strength. Golf is a round of inches and a solitary shot can have the effect of triumph and rout. McIlroy experienced close losses in significant competitions, including season-finisher misfortunes, which expected him to dig profoundly, gain from his missteps, and utilize these difficulties as inspiration to fuel his assurance for future rivalries.

Despite these difficulties and mishaps, Rory McIlroy's capacity to continue, gain from disappointments, and keep up with steadfast self-conviction eventually drove him to significant achievement. Every difficulty turned into a venturing stone, moving him forward on his way to becoming one of the most achieved golf players of his age.

Chapter 4: The Making of a Golfing Legend

Rory McIlroy's journey from a youthful wonder to a genuine legend is downright uncommon. This part digs into the careful creation of his unbelievable status, exploring the components that changed a capable young person into a talented golfer symbol.

Insights into Rory's training and practice routines

Rory McIlroy's progress in proficient golf isn't exclusively ascribed to his regular ability but also to his fastidious preparation and practice schedules. These schedules offer significant bits of knowledge about his way of dealing with the game and what separates him as an elite golf player.

Actual Wellness

Rory McIlroy is known for his extraordinary actual wellness. He consistently works with fitness coaches to guarantee that he is in a top state of being. His preparation incorporates a blend of solidarity preparation, cardiovascular activities, and adaptability work, which are all fundamental for keeping up with the power and endurance expected for golf.

Swing Mechanics

McIlroy's swing is a sight to behold, and it doesn't occur by some coincidence. He goes through innumerable hours refining his swing mechanics with his mentor. His reliable, strong, and in fact, sound swing is a consequence of constant practice and refinement.

Short Game Accuracy: McIlroy's short game is a huge piece of his prosperity. He commits a lot of opportunities to rehearse his putting, chipping, and dugout shots. He deals with his touch and searches the greens, guaranteeing that he can save strokes when it makes the biggest difference.

Mental Strength

Notwithstanding the actual perspectives, McIlroy puts serious areas of strength for mental preparation. He works with sports clinicians to reinforce his psychological distraction, zeroing in on viewpoints like fixation, and flexibility, and keeping a positive mentality on the course.

Reenacted Circumstances

Rory frequently makes recreated competition circumstances during training adjustments. This assists him with planning for high-pressure minutes and fostering systems for different course conditions and situations.

Video Examination

McIlroy utilizes video investigation broadly. He records his swings and audits them with his mentor to recognize regions that need improvement. This logical methodology permits him to make exact changes.

Practice Rounds

Before significant competitions, Rory commonly plays practice adjusts on the competition course to figure out the design, the greens, and the breeze conditions. This nitty-gritty surveillance assists him with concocting his game course of action.

Reiteration and Consistency

McIlroy's hard-working attitude is grounded in consistency. He rehearses consistently, adhering to a thoroughly examined practice plan. This consistency permits him to fabricate muscle memory and keep an elevated degree of execution.

Adaptability

Rory isn't one to adhere to an inflexible daily practice. He adjusts his training and preparation given his exhibition and the particular difficulties he faces. This versatility is critical to his continuous achievement.

Constant Improvement

What separates McIlroy is his tireless drive for development. He never becomes smug with his game, continuously trying to develop and refine his abilities.

His unique style and approach to the game

Rory McIlroy's exceptional style and way of dealing with the sport of golf have been instrumental in laying him out as one of the game's most charming figures. A few viewpoints put him aside from his friends:

Forceful Play

Rory is known for his courageous and forceful style of play. He's not one to avoid any unnecessary risk; all things being equal, he frequently picks forceful shot production, endeavoring to arrive at standard 5 greens in two shots and going after pins. This approach has brought about various stupendous shots and energizing minutes.

Amazing Power

One of McIlroy's characteristics is his amazing power off the tee. He reliably positions among the longest drivers on the PGA Visit. His capacity to send off the ball tremendous distances has given him a critical benefit on many courses, frequently shortening the length of openings for him.

Regular Ability

Rory's swing is in many cases portrayed as a wonderful sight. He has a characteristic, smooth movement that appears to be practically easy. His swing is described by its effortlessness and equilibrium, which empowers him to reliably produce power and exactness.

Mental Strength

While McIlroy is known for his forceful play, he likewise keeps major areas of strength for a game. He doesn't harp on botches and can return from difficulties.

This psychological versatility played an urgent impact on his prosperity.

Versatility

Rory isn't restricted to a solitary style or procedure. He adjusts his game to various courses and conditions. His flexibility permits him to perform well in different settings, be it a connections-style course with an eccentric climate or a customary parkland course.

Constant Improvement

McIlroy's obligation to personal growth is obvious all through his profession. He reliably looks to refine his abilities and calibrate his way of dealing with the game. This devotion to progress has prompted his predictable presence at the highest point of hitting the fairway world.

Impact on the world of golf

Rory McIlroy's effect on the universe of golf is significant and expansive, making him perhaps the most powerful figure in the game. His commitments range in different parts of golf, including the following:

Worldwide Motivation

Rory McIlroy's extraordinary journey from a little fellow in Northern Ireland to a four-time significant boss has motivated endless hopeful golf players around the world. His story fills in as a demonstration of the potential outcomes inside the game, propelling youthful ability to seek after their fantasies.

Youth Commitment

Rory has been an area of strength for getting youngsters engaged with golf. His Rory Establishment, which upholds youngsters' causes, advances golf as an instrument for positive change. He's assumed an essential part in making golf more open to youth and underserved networks.

Specialized Development

McIlroy's extraordinary style and procedure have impacted golf guidance. His strong yet controlled swing has turned into a subject of study for the two beginners and experts, meaningfully having an impact on how golf players approach their game.

Execution Norms

Rory's consistency in high-stakes competitions and his surprising ball-striking have set new guidelines for execution. He has moved different golf players to raise their game, adding to the consistently expanding seriousness of expert golf.

Worldwide Ambassadorship

As a worldwide envoy for golf, Rory McIlroy's presence has developed the game's prevalence universally. His support on occasions overall has extended golf's range and presented it to assorted crowds.

The Cutting edge Golf player

McIlroy's persona as an interesting, practical competitor has modernized golf's picture. His utilization of web-based entertainment and congenial disposition make him a good example for the up-and-coming age of players and fans.

Beneficent Effect

Through his magnanimous endeavors, Rory has demonstrated the way that golf players can have a huge effect on the planet. His commitments to different causes have featured the empathetic side of expert competitors, empowering charity inside the golf local area.

Chapter 5: Life Off the Course

While Rory McIlroy's life on the green is factual and commended, it is similarly interesting to explore his life away from the fairways.

Rory's personal life, relationships, and hobbies

Rory McIlroy's own life, connections, and side interests offer a brief look into the man behind the playing golf legend. Here is a concise exploration of these viewpoints:

Individual Life:

Rory McIlroy, despite his gigantic outcome in golf, has consistently kept a rational and receptive disposition. He was brought into the world on May 4, 1989, in Hollywood, Northern Ireland. His childhood was affectionate, and his family played a huge part in sustaining his energy for golf. McIlroy's dad, Gerry, maintained numerous sources of income to help his child's golf desires, in any event, functioning as a barman at Holywood Golf Club.

Rory's own life has been set apart by areas of strength for his foundations and his country, Northern Ireland. He remains intently attached to his local area and has upheld different worthy missions in the district.

Relationships:

In 2012, Rory McIlroy became connected with tennis star Caroline Wozniacki, however, the commitment finished before their arranged wedding. McIlroy's next section saw him marry Erica Stoll, an American lady who worked for the PGA of

America. Their wedding in 2017 was a special arrangement, mirroring McIlroy's longing to get a few parts of his life far from the public eye.

Rory's relationship with Erica has been a steady and stable presence in his life. They have shared their encounters venturing to the far corners of the planet and encountering the ups and downs of elite athletics.

Hobbies:

While golf rules a lot of Rory's expert life, he likewise has a scope of leisure activities and interests outside the game. One of his outstanding leisure activities is his adoration for soccer (football), especially his help for Manchester United. McIlroy has periodically been seen going to football matches and supporting his #1 group.

Apart from sports, Rory loves Formula 1 racing and is known to go to races when his timetable permits. He's likewise a wine fan, having sent off his wine image, "Rory McIlroy, The Collection," which includes a choice of wines.

These leisure activities give equilibrium to McIlroy's life, permitting him to unwind and appreciate interests past the green. They exhibit the different and multi-layered character of a golf player who has accomplished a lot but remains profoundly associated with his own life, connections, and interests.

His philanthropic efforts and contributions

Rory McIlroy, famous for his ability on the fairway, is similarly great off the greens because of his significant generous endeavors and commitments. Through his Rory Establishment, laid out in 2013, McIlroy has shown a profound obligation to have a beneficial outcome on the existences of others.

One of McIlroy's critical altruistic undertakings centers around kids' causes. His establishment upholds kids' foundations, expecting to give better medical care, schooling, and open doors for oppressed youth. McIlroy's obligation to this cause has prompted the subsidizing of different tasks and drives all over the planet, guaranteeing that kids in need approach fundamental administrations and instructive assets.

As well as supporting kids' foundations, McIlroy has been effectively engaged with advancing disease exploration and treatment. He has made significant gifts to malignant growth places and examination associations, adding to the continuous endeavors to track down successful medicines and eventually a remedy for this overwhelming sickness.

His magnanimous commitments reach out to calamity aid ventures. He has given alleviation assets for catastrophic events, giving genuinely necessary guidance to networks impacted by storms, quakes, and different disasters. His help has helped these networks remake and recuperate, exhibiting his sympathy for those confronting affliction.

Besides, McIlroy has been a serious area of strength for training. He puts stock in the force of information to change lives and has upheld different instructive drives, including grant programs and instructive foundations. By putting resources into schooling, McIlroy is enabling people to break hindrances and accomplish their maximum capacity.

Through his altruistic undertakings, he has made significant monetary commitments as well as brought issues to light about significant social issues. His commitment to making a positive effect mirrors his faith in capitalizing on his leverage to improve society. Subsequently, he keeps on rousing others, both inside and outside the universe of golf, to contribute seriously to the prosperity of mankind.

Balancing fame and privacy

Adjusting notoriety and protection is a sensitive tightrope walk, particularly for well-known individuals like Rory McIlroy.

In a period where online entertainment enhances each part of an individual's life, finding harmony between an effective profession in the public eye and a confidential life can be challenging.

Keeping an Individual Space

One of the essential battles looked at by superstars is the intrusion of individual space. Consistent media consideration and public assessment can make it hard to appreciate regular exercise without undesirable consideration. Basic assignments like shopping for food or eating out become public scenes, making it fundamental for people like McIlroy to cut out private, untouchable spaces where they can unwind without depending on the world.

Protecting Connections

Famous people frequently track down their connections under serious investigation. For Rory McIlroy, his close connections have much of the time stood out as truly newsworthy. Keeping a steady private life amid media is genuinely drained. Safeguarding the righteousness of connections requires deliberate work to protect them from the intrusive idea of distinction.

Defining Limits

It is vital to Lay out clear limits. This could mean restricting the openness of one's very own life via web-based entertainment or being particular about open appearances. McIlroy, in the same way as other VIPs, possibly picks when and where to be in the public eye, permitting him to offset his expert commitments with his requirement for security.

Taking care of Online Entertainment

Virtual entertainment stages offer a situation with two sides for superstars. While they furnish an immediate channel of correspondence with fans, they likewise open individual lives to a tremendous crowd. McIlroy, known for his dynamic presence via virtual entertainment, logically explores this space cautiously, sharing parts of his life while defending what is private.

Adapting to Bits of Hypothesis

The gossip plant is an inescapable piece of notoriety. Misleading stories can strain individual connections and cause profound pain. It requires areas of strength to disregard ridiculous stereotypes and spotlight on reality, while not allowing cynicism to influence individual prosperity.

Keeping up with Credibility

In the time of organized public pictures, it is trying to remain consistent with oneself. Legitimacy can be eclipsed by the craving to measure up to public assumptions. McIlroy's capacity to offset his public persona with his certified self probably includes remaining consistent with his qualities and not surrendering to outer tensions, guaranteeing that his public picture lines up with his genuine character.

Chapter 6: Triumphs and Trials

In the emotional ride that is Rory McIlroy's celebrated hitting the fairway career, we will dive deep into the many triumphs and preliminaries he has confronted. From the most elevated of highs to the least of lows, this part investigates mind-boggling strength and assurance that have characterized McIlroy as a golf player and an individual.

Reflecting on career highs and lows

Pondering the ups and downs is a vital part of grasping the golf player as well as the person behind the putter. It is an excursion set apart by both euphoria and despondency, and it gives priceless experiences into the mind of a top-notch competitor.

The Highs:

Significant Triumphs

The apex of Rory McIlroy's career has been his significant title wins. The U.S. Open in 2011 and The Open Championship in 2014, among others, were pivotal occasions. These triumphs exhibited his uncommon ability and showed his capacity to perform under massive tension.

World No. 1

There were periods when McIlroy ruled as the world's highest-level golf player. These snapshots of strength featured his consistency and capacity to support maximum execution over overstretched periods.

Record-Breaking Rounds

Rory's capacity to establish course standards and post-striking rounds of golf has been a demonstration of his inconceivable expertise and assurance. These rounds frequently came at crucial points in time of competitions.

The Lows:

Injury Mishaps

Rory McIlroy, in the same way as other competitors, needed to confront the test of wounds. In 2015, he experienced a lower leg injury, which affected his exhibition. These mishaps tried his flexibility and persistence.

Expert Tragedy

The Bosses is a competition that Rory has been near winning, however, it has escaped him up until this point. The close misses and the extreme strain of seeking the tricky green coat have been troublesome minutes in his vocation.

Battles with Structure

Rory's career likewise saw periods where he battled with his structure. The disappointment of not fulfilling his high guidelines and the assumptions of fans and the media weighed vigorously on him.

The Reflection:

Thinking about these ups and downs, Rory McIlroy has shown remarkable beauty and strength. He has been open about his battles, which has charmed him to fans significantly more. Every difficulty has gone about as an impetus for him to return more grounded, while every triumph has built up his self-conviction.

What stands apart most in this reflection is that Rory McIlroy's journey, similar to any extraordinary competitor's, is a mix of taking off triumphs and lowering losses. It's a demonstration of the human soul's ability to persevere, adjust, and adapt to new situations. It is at these times of reflection that we are the golf player as well as the individual behind the golf player's persona, somebody who faces life's difficulties here and there on the course with splendid assurance and character.

The mental and physical challenges of professional golf

Proficient golf is a game that requests a novel mix of mental and actual ability. The psychological and actual difficulties faced by golf players, including somebody as accomplished as Rory McIlroy, are vital to their prosperity and life span in the game.

Mental Difficulties:

Fixation and Concentration

Golf requires serious fixation. Golf players should keep up with the entry for extended periods, now and again north of five hours of play, to make exact shots and read the greens. Interruptions, self-uncertainty, or nervousness can wreck a round.

Strain and Assumptions

The heaviness of assumptions, both individual and from fans, backers, and media, can be tremendous. Significant competitions frequently accompany uplifted strain, and golf players should figure out how to reverse it.

Course The executives

Smartness is vital for choosing the right shot, overseeing dangers, and figuring out the course's subtleties. Unfortunate choices can bring about extra strokes.

Consistency

Golf players make progress toward consistency in their swings, putts, and mental states. The psychological test lies in rehashing effective shots and procedures under differing conditions.

Actual Difficulties:

Endurance

Playing a series of golf, particularly in an expert setting, requires critical perseverance. Golf players walk a few miles during a round and make many swings, which can truly be a burden.

Injury Anticipation

Golf players are inclined to different wounds, especially toward the back, wrists, and shoulders, because of the dull idea of the game. Remaining in great shape is critical to executing injury avoidance procedures.

Weather patterns

Golf players should battle with different weather patterns, from burning intensity to weighty downpours Adjusting to these circumstances and remaining agreeable is an actual test.

Strength and Adaptability

Developing fortitude and adaptability is fundamental for creating power and executing various sorts of shots. Golf players participate in strength preparation and customary extending schedules to work on their game.

For somebody like Rory McIlroy, who has arrived at the zenith of expert golf, dominating these moves has been vital to his prosperity. Mental versatility and actual wellness have permitted him to perform reliably at the most elevated level and quickly return from mishaps.

Comebacks and resilience in the face of adversity

All through his celebrated hitting the fairway profession, Rory McIlroy has been no more peculiar to misfortune. His excursion to becoming one of the game's most notable figures has been set apart by promising and less promising times, including mishaps and difficulties that tested his versatility. What separates McIlroy, be that as it may, is his noteworthy capacity to organize rebounds and defeat difficulty, arising more grounded and more resolved each time.

Injury and Setbacks

Perhaps the main test Rory confronted was injury. In 2015, he experienced a burst lower leg tendon while playing soccer, which took steps to crash his profession. The accident caused him to miss key competitions, including The Open Championship. In any case, Rory's assurance to recuperate and get back to the highest point of his game was immovable. He recuperated as well as returned considerably more grounded, winning numerous competitions before long.

The Bosses Heartbreak

Rory McIlroy's quest for a career Huge Grand Slam in golf made them battle for the sought-after Green Jacket at The Experts. He came excruciatingly close in 2011 yet floundered during the last round. The failure might have wrecked numerous players, yet

McIlroy involved it as inspiration. He exhibited massive mental versatility and, in 2012, got his most memorable significant triumph at the PGA Title. His awfulness eventually filled his rebound and further achievement.

Dunks in Structure

Like all competitors, Rory has encountered variances in his exhibition. There were periods when his structure disappeared, and pundits scrutinized his capacities. During these times, McIlroy showed his versatility by working tenaciously to tweak his game. He made fundamental changes, looked for the direction of mentors, and tried harder and by. These rebounds from execution lows help us to remember his relentless obligation to greatness.

Mental Sturdiness

McIlroy's capacity to keep a cool head under tension is a demonstration of his psychological determination. Whether it's a high-stakes significant title or a basic putt on the last opening, he figures out how to keep on track and perform at his best. His psychological flexibility has been essential in his rebound triumphs and capacity to beat testing circumstances on the fairway.

Motivation to Other people

Rory McIlroy's journey of rebounds and strength fills in as a motivation to many hopeful golf players and people confronting difficulty in their own lives. He exhibits that misfortunes are essential for the excursion to progress, and the key is to continue pushing forward, gaining from botches, and never abandoning one's objectives.

Rory McIlroy's story is a demonstration of the force of strength and assurance in the realm of sports. His rebounds even with misfortune not only set his status as a playing golf legend yet in addition act as a wellspring of inspiration for anybody hoping to conquer difficulties and accomplish their fantasies. Through McIlroy's journey, we see that misfortunes are not road obstructions; they are potential open doors for a victorious re-visitation of significance.

Chapter 7: Rory McIlroy's Enduring Legacy

As a hitting the fairway legend, McIlroy's inheritance extends a long way past the limits of the green, making a permanent imprint on the game and rousing ages to come.

Rory's impact on the sport of golf

Rory McIlroy, with his striking ability, relentless assurance, and irresistible charm, has made a permanent imprint on the game of golf. His effect reverberates not just through his phenomenal accomplishments on the course but also in the manner he has enlivened another age of golf players and enthralled fans around the world.

1. Rejuvenating the Game

McIlroy burst onto the expert golf scene with an energy and excitement that attracted fans who probably wouldn't have been keen on the game previously. His dynamic style of play, described by strong drives and exact putting, infused new energy into golf, making it more interesting to more youthful crowds.

2. Global Symbol

Hailing from Northern Ireland, McIlroy's prosperity globalized the game. He turned into a signal for hopeful golf players outside the customary golf forces to be reckoned with, demonstrating that ability knows no limits. His worldwide allure extended golf's compass, making it a worldwide game.

3. Sportsmanship and Moxy

McIlroy's sportsmanship and real disposition have charmed him to fans around the world. His charitableness in both triumph and rout sets a model for yearning golf players, underscoring the significance of lowliness and regard in the game. His cooperation with fans, both on and off the course, has made areas of strength for an aim and the playing golf local area.

4. Charitable Commitments

Past his accomplishments, McIlroy has made huge commitments off the course. He laid out the Rory Establishment, a beneficent association pointed toward aiding kids out of luck. His generous endeavors have displayed the positive impact competitors can have on society, rousing others in the games world to offer in return.

5. Moving the Future

McIlroy's example of overcoming adversity fills in as a wellspring of motivation for youthful golf players around the world. His excursion from a skilled youthful novice to a different time-significant boss propels hopeful players to perseveringly seek after their fantasies. He effectively draws in with youth drives, tutoring, and supporting youthful gifts, guaranteeing the progression of golf's heritage.

6. Setting New Principles

McIlroy's accomplishments have set new norms for greatness in golf. His record-breaking exhibitions, remembering his coming out on top for numerous significant titles, have increased present expectations for what golf players can accomplish. Hopeful players presently admire McIlroy as a benchmark of progress, endeavoring to coordinate and surpass his achievements.

His Great influence on future generations of golfers

Rory McIlroy's impact on people in the future of golf players is significant and multi-layered. As one of the game's most gifted and alluring figures, he has made a permanent imprint on the universe of golf, rousing youthful players in various ways:

Specialized Authority

McIlroy's flawless swing and generally speaking specialized greatness have turned into a model for trying golf players. His consistency and accuracy in ball striking act as a kind of perspective point for youthful players hoping to consummate their strategies.

Mental Durability

Rory's capacity to deal with the tensions of expert golf has procured his titles as well as been a wellspring of motivation for those needing to work on their psychological distraction. His self-restraint in high-pressure circumstances fills in as a sign of the significance of mental strength in golf.

Worldwide Viewpoint

As a global golf player, Rory's prosperity has risen above borders. His worldwide allure has empowered hopeful golf players from all edges of the world, cultivating a more different and comprehensive hitting of the fairway local area.

Youth Improvement

McIlroy's establishment and magnanimous endeavors have upheld youth advancement in golf. His obligation to give access and open doors to youthful golf players has opened entryways for the future.

Physicality and Wellness

McIlroy's emphasis on wellness and physicality has acquainted another aspect of the game. His devotion to functional preparation has roused youthful golf players to focus on well-being and wellness as fundamental parts of their hitting the fairway venture.

Incredible skill and Sportsmanship

Rory McIlroy is known for his incredible skill and sportsmanship on and off the course. His direction sets an elevated requirement for youthful players, stressing the significance of regard, fair play, and modesty in the game.

Altruistic Drives

Through his magnanimous undertakings, Rory has demonstrated the way that competitors can involve their foundation for positive change. Youthful golf players are motivated by their on-course accomplishments as well as by their obligation to reward the local area.

Generational Extension

McIlroy's capacity to associate with both more established and more youthful golf fans helps span generational holes. Youthful golf players can gain from the customs of the game while embracing its advancement.

Rory McIlroy's impact on people in the future of golf players expands well past his triumphs and records. His effect is portrayed by his specialized ability, mental flexibility, worldwide reach, and obligation to the improvement of youthful ability. He fills in as a good example for youthful golf players

Speculation on what the future holds for this golfing legend

For Rory McIlroy, it is based on his capability to solidify his heritage as one of golf's unsurpassed greats. Starting around 2021, McIlroy had previously made striking progress in the game, yet many golf fans and specialists trust that there's something else to come.

One huge part of his future is the quest for the Championship. McIlroy has shown over and over that he has what it takes, insight, and mental strength to battle in significant competitions. Golf devotees enthusiastically expect the chance for him to add to his generally amazing significant title count. The subtle journey for a lifelong Huge homerun, where a golf player wins every one of the four significant Championship, was something that energized fans. The tempting possibility of Rory McIlroy joining this selective club was a consistent subject of conversation.

Besides, McIlroy's effect on the game reaches out past his hitting the fairway capacities. His initiative, sportsmanship, and humanitarian endeavors have proactively made him a good example for the overwhelming majority of trying golf players. Hypothesis frequently spun around how he could proceed to motivate and impact the up-and-coming age of golf players and reward the game.

Questions additionally emerged about his life span and the chance of him proceeding to contend at the most elevated level into his forties and then some. McIlroy's wellness routine and devotion to his specialty were viewed as markers that he could lastingly influence the game.

At last, what was in store held the commitment of new records, moving accomplishments, and the continuous impact of hitting the fairway legend. Be that as it may, explicit results and achievements would rely upon his proceedings with devotion, well-being, and execution on the fairway.

Conclusion

Rory McIlroy's journey through the universe of golf is phenomenal. From his humble starting points as a young man in Northern Ireland to becoming one of the most prestigious and achieved golf players of his age, his story is a demonstration of devotion, ability, and unfaltering enthusiasm. With a wonderful profession set apart by numerous significant titles, unfaltering assurance, and a veritable love for the game, McIlroy has not just made a permanent imprint on the fairways yet in addition in the hearts of fans around the world.

Past his expertise on the fairway, McIlroy's personality and trustworthiness have made him a good example for hopeful competitors and a wellspring of motivation for people who face misfortune. He has exhibited that with difficult work, versatility, and a solid emotionally supportive network, dreams can for sure be transformed into the real world.

As Rory McIlroy keeps on developing both his expert and individual life, his heritage perseveres as an image of greatness in the realm of golf. His story advises us that with immovable devotion, even the loftiest of objectives can be accomplished. Whether you're a golf player or an admirer of an exceptional journey, Rory McIlroy's story starts with getting through the soul of human accomplishment and the quest for significance.

Printed in Great Britain
by Amazon

33666233R00050